A LIGHT TO SHARE

Stories of Spreading Love and Changing the World

Written by Natalie Frisk

Illustrated by María Diaz Perera

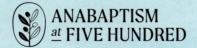

Harrisonburg, Virginia

Hey. Hey, you! Yes, YOU! I've got a question for you:

Have you ever gotten a really great present from someone who loves you?

And then . . . you realize that if you share that gift, it is even better than you thought?

God does that for us, you know.
God gives us really amazing gifts.

God loves you so much and knows you so well. God is the best gift-giver. And when God gives us gifts—like being science-smart or creative or a good friend—it's even better when we share our gifts with others!

When we discover our gifts from God, it is like a light flips on inside us. I'd like to tell you about 12 friends of God who shared their light with the world around them!

Meet Conrad Grebel. Say, "Hi, Conrad!"

When Conrad was your age, he wasn't one of the best students.

He had a hard time with some of the learning.

He had a hard time with some of the people.

He had a hard time figuring out what he should do next.

Then Conrad joined a Bible study, and he realized he liked learning about Jesus! Jesus said, "Love your neighbor," and "Love your enemy" too. Conrad liked talking about these big ideas.

This was when the light flipped on inside Conrad. Conrad helped other people know more about Jesus' teaching, and he became the creator of a new community of people who were following Jesus as best they could. They were called Anabaptists!

Meet Helena von Freyberg. Say, "Hi, Helena!"

When Helena was your age, she lived in a castle in the country of Austria. Yes, a castle!

Helena and her family and all the people in her town had to follow rules about going to church. There were things you were allowed to say and do, and things you were not allowed to say and do. One big rule said you had to be baptized as a baby.

Helena heard about some people who were choosing to be baptized as grown-ups. How strange, she must have thought. But then she met them, and the light flipped on for Helena.

Helena decided that *she* wanted to be baptized as a grown-up to show everyone she wanted to follow Jesus forever! And even though she could have gotten in big trouble, Helena let this group of Jesus followers have church at her house—well, castle. Her light was shining bright.

Meet Christoph Sauer. Say, "Hi, Christoph!"

When Christoph was your age, he lived in the country of Germany and spoke German.

As an adult, Christoph moved to the United States. He worked as a tailor, a clockmaker, a farmer, and a surgeon. He also learned to print books.

Do you know how they used to make books, before computers? A printer like Christoph would line up tiny letter blocks to spell out all the words on a page, then cover those letters with ink to print a page—like a big stamp on paper! Each book took loads of time.

Christoph thought about people who wanted to read the Bible in German. That's when the light flipped on inside Christoph! Christoph printed the first German Bible in North America. *Danke*—thank you—Christoph!

Meet Tunggul Wulung. Say, "Hi, Tunggul!"

The story of Tunggul's childhood is a mystery! He is from an island country now called Indonesia, where some people think he was a member of the royal family. (Prince Tunggul?) Or he was on the run for stealing a horse. (Thief Tunggul?) Or he was a rebel. (Fighter Tunggul?)

But no matter who Tunggul was when he was younger, his life changed when he met a woman named Endang who was interested in God. Tunggul also discovered a copy of the Ten Commandments that mysteriously appeared under his sleeping mat. And Tunggul and Endang liked talking about Jesus together.

And that is when the light flipped on in Tunggul! Tunggul became a follower of Jesus and shared the light of Jesus with people all over his island of Java!

Meet Anna Mow. Say, "Hi, Anna!"

When Anna was your age, she lived with her mom, dad, brother, and *many* sisters. They loved learning, playing games, and laughing a lot! Anna's family prayed together every day. Anna followed Jesus with her whole life.

One day, the light flipped on in Anna that God wanted her to become a missionary—that's someone who is "on a mission" for God, sharing the good news message of Jesus!

Anna went to the country of India as a missionary. People in India were surprised by how welcoming and kind Anna was to them. You see, in India at that time, people were not equal. In most cases, wealthy people were not friends with poor people. People with different skin colors did not hang out. It was not fair!

Anna rebelled with kindness and welcomed all people to be her friend. She learned from the Indian people, too. This helped her in her faith in Jesus. And Anna shared the light of Jesus everywhere she went!

Meet Edna Ruth Byler.
Say, "Hi, Edna Ruth!"

When Edna Ruth was your age, she went to church and learned of God's love for all people.

As an adult, Edna Ruth traveled to the island of Puerto Rico. There she met some women who didn't have enough money to feed their children. But she also saw that the women created beautiful fabric arts—and that's when the light flipped on for Edna Ruth! She decided to gather the women's handiwork and sell it out of the trunk of her car after she traveled home. This meant that the women could buy food for their families! Hooray!

Edna Ruth's idea grew . . . and grew! For the next 30 years, Edna Ruth found artists in countries all over the world and set up ways to sell their items. The organization that Edna Ruth started is now called Ten Thousand Villages. High five, Edna Ruth! Or—ten thousand high fives!

Meet Alta Schrock. Say, "Hi, Alta!"

When Alta was your age, she didn't go to school, because she was sick ALL. THE. TIME! But Alta wanted to learn cool stuff. So she would go out into the woods and study the plants around her home.

This was when the light flipped on in Alta.

Alta loved learning about all the life that God had made.

When Alta was a teenager, she was *finally* able to go to school with other kids.

She went on to college to learn about biology—that's the study of living things!

Alta became an expert in biology and a kind of teacher called a professor. She got to teach about the amazing world of living things that God had made!

Doctor Alta (as she became known) shared her light by helping people discover how to take care of God's creation! Thanks, Dr. Alta!

Meet Lawrence Homer Hart, also known as Sky Chief. Say, "Hi, Sky Chief!"

When Lawrence was your age, he helped his family earn money by working in the fields. While he did this, he would see airplanes fly by. Lawrence decided that one day, he would fly!

At age 17, Lawrence decided to follow Jesus. Some time later, he also learned how to fly jets! Lawrence's grandfather was a peace chief of the Cheyenne. When Lawrence's grandfather died, it was decided that Lawrence would take his place. Lawrence got to fly a jet back to his home for his ceremony to become chief.

That day, he was given the name He'amavehonevėstse, or Sky Chief, and his light truly shone bright. Sky Chief was a peace chief for the Cheyenne, and he became a pastor in a Mennonite church. He helped share the good news message of Jesus with the Cheyenne and with other people as well. Sky Chief shared his light as a peacemaker.

Meet Paulus Hartono. Say, "Hi, Paulus!"

When Paulus was your age, he didn't yet know Jesus. He knew that God was real, and he wanted to follow God. One day, someone told Paulus about Jesus! That's when the light flipped on in Paulus, and he soon became a pastor.

In Paulus's country, Indonesia, Muslims and Christians didn't get along. But Paulus knew that Jesus wants us to love our enemies! So he decided to make friends with a man whom the local Christians feared the most.

Paulus and this man, Yanni, learned to listen to each other. And do you know what? They became good friends!

Soon after, a tsunami hit—that's a series of extra-large waves from the ocean—and it caused thousands of people to lose their homes. Paulus and Yanni decided to team up to help as many people as they could!

Meet Issa Ebombolo. Say, "Hi, Issa!"

When Issa was your age, he moved from the country of Burundi to the Congo. His family had been refugees—a refugee is someone who must leave their home because it is unsafe. For Issa's family, it was because of war.

When they arrived in the Congo, Issa went to school. Issa loved learning, and he decided to become a teacher. As a grown-up, Issa learned about Jesus. He said YES to following Jesus forever! (*Wahoo!*)

Sadly, Issa's country was at war again. He moved to *another* country, Zambia. That's when the light flipped on in Issa!

Issa knew that being a peacemaker was important to God.

He knew he could help make peace!

Issa started peace clubs at schools to help teach kids and grown-ups how to be kind, speak calmly, and live peacefully. Issa's idea grew and grew. Now, there are peace clubs all over Africa, in Canada, and in South America!

Meet Kate Bowler. Say, "Hi, Kate!"

When Kate was your age, her parents were professors at a university. Kate loved learning. She went to college and got not one, not two, but three degrees (that's a lot of school!) and became a history professor like her dad!

As a grown-up, Kate got a really difficult kind of cancer. The doctors didn't know if she would live very long. Kate was so sad because she had a happy life. How could this happen?

Even though it was terrible, something incredible happened too. The light flipped on in Kate! She wrote books about God, her life, and having cancer. And people loved reading them because her honesty helped others share their feelings. Kate started a podcast, and her light shines brightly through it too. And do you know what? Even though Kate's experience sounds kind of sad, she has one of the most joyful podcasts around!

Meet Drew G. I. Hart. Say, "Hi, Drew!"

When Drew was your age, he loved to play basketball with his brother. Drew's family loved following Jesus together. As a teenager, Drew felt God inviting him to become a pastor. That's when the light flipped on in Drew. He said YES! to God's invitation.

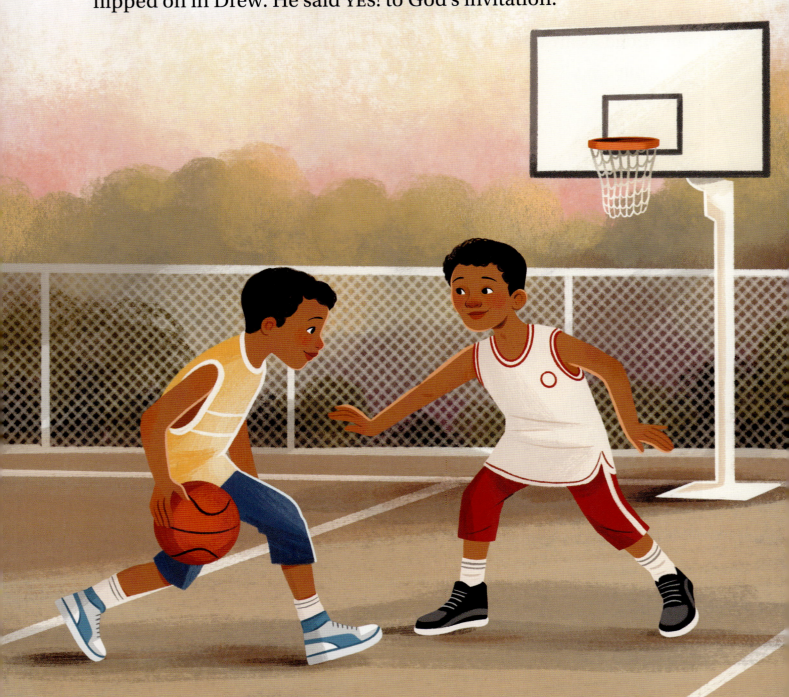

One day, Drew got a phone call telling him that his brother had been arrested. But his brother hadn't done anything wrong. The police had been looking for a young Black man in a T-shirt. And his brother happened to be wearing a T-shirt and was young and had dark skin. This was not fair! This was part of a big problem called racism—that is treating someone unkindly or unfairly because of the color of their skin—and is not part of the way of Jesus.

Drew kept studying and earned a big degree called a doctorate, so now he is Dr. Drew! And Dr. Drew shines his light by teaching others and peacefully fighting against things that are unfair, like racism.

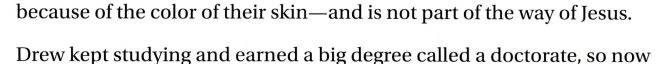

All of these people have one person in common. Can you guess who? It's Jesus!

Say, "Hi, Jesus!"

When Jesus was your age, he lived with his parents Mary and Joseph and his younger siblings.

When he was 30 years old, Jesus began his ministry: telling people all about God's loving kingdom. Jesus invited others to come and follow and learn from him.

Jesus said, "I am the light of the world." He's the light that flips on inside of us, and his Holy Spirit is the gift we receive that helps us share his light everywhere we go! And guess what? Jesus also said, "You are the light of the world!" Jesus is playing the best game of tag ever! He's saying, "You've got my light now. Go share it with everyone!"

So, tag—you're it! How will you share the light?

*To Erin, Sloane, Knox, Will, Felicity, and Wren.
May God ignite the light in each of you.
I can't wait to see how it shines!*
—**NF**

*To my lovely mother
for always being the guiding light of my life.*
—**MDP**

Herald Press
PO Box 866, Harrisonburg, Virginia 22803
www.HeraldPress.com

Library of Congress cataloging-in-publication data has been applied for.

A LIGHT TO SHARE
© 2025 by Herald Press, Harrisonburg, Virginia 22803. 800-245-7894.
   All rights reserved.
Library of Congress Control Number: 2024017916
International Standard Book Number: 978-1-5138-1446-9 (hardcover);
   978-1-5138-1447-6 (ebook)

Printed in China

All rights reserved. This publication may not be reproduced, stored in a retrieval system, or transmitted in whole or in part, in any form, by any means, electronic, mechanical, photocopying, recording or otherwise without prior permission of the copyright owners.

29 28 27 26 25   10 9 8 7 6 5 4 3 2 1

The Author and Illustrator

Natalie Frisk has worked in ministry for over 15 years. She earned a master's in theological study and is pursing a doctorate in practical theology with an emphasis on the spiritual experience of children. While she was the curriculum pastor for a multisite church, Natalie published *Raising Disciples: How to Make Faith Matter for Our Kids*. She is now director of curriculum for RaiseUpFaith. She is married to Sam and mom to Erin.

María Diaz Perera was born in Gijón, a small seaside town in northern Spain. When she was very young, she found out that there were few things in life that she enjoyed as much as listening to the Beatles and drawing. She graduated with a degree in art history, and soon after that she studied graphic design. María has worked as a freelance illustrator for several international publishers, magazines, and advertising agencies, and she loves to work on portraits and children's books. She is very inspired by music from the 1960s and 1970s, as well as literature and cinema, and she loves to spend time with family and friends. She still listens to the Beatles and feels fortunate to be able to do what she loves the most for a living: illustration.